MORAL EDUCATION STUDIES

A FAMILY LIFE EDUCATION (FLE) STUDENT'S
WORKBOOK FOR UPPER PRIMARY
AND JUNIOR SECONDARY PUPILS

HABIBAT ONYIOZA SHEIDU

Order this book online at www.trafford.com
or email orders@trafford.com

Most Trafford titles are also available at major online book retailers.

Illustrations by Marybeth Neff

Print information available on the last page.

ISBN: 978-1-4907-5076-7 (sc)

Trafford rev. 02/25/2017

Trafford
PUBLISHING®   www.trafford.com
North America & international
toll-free: 1 888 232 4444 (USA & Canada)
fax: 812 355 4082

CONTENTS

Habibat Onyioza Sheidu is one of the Corps Member who volunteered to be a development worker taking the message of the NYSC/MDG Family Life Education to the communities in the Federal capital territory (FCT)

She stood out amongst her colleagues by leaving an indelible mark in the sands of time through the publication of this book which demonstrates her commitment to the issues of family life Education and her obvious love for her host community that places a high premium on sound morals as an engine of a greater Nigeria of our dreams.

She displayed her vast knowledge of the subject matter in bringing out the issues of Family life Education in a simple and easily comprehensible manner for the upper primary and lower secondary school pupils.

Even though this workbook was patterned after the NYSC Family Life Education Manual, the workbook gives opportunity for increased participation of the students and presents issues from their stand point such that they can easily relate to it.

Habibat Onyioza Sheidu's contribution is no doubt unique and considering the meager allowance of corps members, it is certainly a great sacrifice to humanity and the Nigerian Children that has resulted in the production of this book.

Though it is said that the cover of a book does not determine its contents I make bold to say that the beautiful cover of this book also indicate the depth of knowledge, arrangement of fact and carefully planned topics put together for moral studies suitable for higher primary and lower secondary school pupils.

This book is recommended for the use of pupils of the upper primary and lower secondary schools as well as other concerned stakeholders

Mrs S.I.E Omokri
Director,
Community Development Services Department
NYSC DHQ Abuja
2007

I am honored to write the foreword to a Family Life Education. This is a workbook that is both timely and relevant. It provides valuable information while seeking to address the core values that we as Nigerians seem to have lost over time.

It is a book that has great utility for schools nationwide as well as community groups working with children. Family with its central placement as the first group that we know has implications on how we relate to groups of the society

This book goes a long way to teach children how to function within the family and within the society at large. It tackles issues that are sensitive but pertinent to all children in a way that is compassionate and accessible

It is a book that I recommend for all those who work with children

Yours Faithfully,
Dr. Fatima Akilu
Communications Expert OSSAP-MDGs
2007

DEDICATION

This work is dedicated to all children who will imbibe the sound morals learnt from this book.

ACKNOWLEDGEMENTS

My profound gratitude goes to the following:

I. My dad, Saka Sheidu for always encouraging me to write.

II. Prof. Tahir Gidado, his interest in this book and potent words of encouragement remains invigorating to me for life.

III. Staff of the National institute for Pharmaceutical research and Development (NIPRD) Idu Abuja; Dr Ufot S. Inyang, Dr.O. O Kunle, Dr. O. Obodozie, Dr. Victoria Eyo, Pharm. Martins Emeje, Mr. David Akanwa and Mrs Justina Iyagba. The depth of knowledge they imparted on me during my internship and service year is sustaining me till now. I also thank them for creating such an amiable working environment without which it would have been impossible for me to write this book.

IV. My friends Kunle Ogundele and Kunle Lawal for their technical expertise

V. Assessors at the Nigerian Educational Research and development council (NERDC) for all the reviews.

INTRODUCTION

Children aged 5 to 14 represent a window of opportunity to a HIV free society. 'Catching them young' and making a difference is our aim in the Family Life Education community development group.

This book is intended to serve as a workbook for pupils aged 7 to 14 years who are thought the

Family Life education Modules.

It serves as a guide as well as a means of evaluating the impact of training.

Kingsely Musa,
Family Life Education Schedule Officer
NYSC Abuja.
2007

Name of student

Age

Sex

Class

State of origin

Religion

Home Address

Phone number

Number of brothers (list names)

Number of sisters (list names)

Number of friends (list names)

Languages spoken

Date course commenced   Date course ended

CHAPTER ONE

1.0   INTRODUCTION TO FAMILY LIFE:

Activity
Place your family picture here

1.1   DEFINATION OF A FAMILY

A family is the smallest unit of a community. It is usually the first agent of socialization a child encounters in life. Different families make up a community, different communities make a society and different societies a country.

1.2   TYPES OF FAMILY

A family consists of 'parents and children' with or without relatives. Types of family include the nuclear family and the extended family.

Activity:
What are the types of families you know? List and explain each

....
....
....

....
....
....
....

....
....
....
....
....
....

Can we conclude that a family is a group of people living together in the same house? Tick your answer.

YES [   ]   NO [   ]
Give reasons for your answer:

....
....
....
....
....
....
....
....
....

1.3   IMPORTANCE OF A GOOD FAMILY

1.3.1   A GOOD FAMILY MAKES A BETTER SOCIETY

The importance of a family cannot be overemphasized because a family is the most important aspect of any society. A good family results in a good society while a bad family leads to problems or vices in our society.

Activity:
List some societal ills you know

....
....
....
....
....
....
....

1.3.2 A GOOD FAMILY PROVIDES FOR YOUR NEEDS

Most of our human needs can be provided for by our families.

Activity:
What do you understand by human needs?

....
....
....
....
....
....
....

It is very important to note that **only** your family can provide all your needs unconditionally. Asking other people apart from members of your family can cause you difficulties because they may take advantage of you.

Activity
a. What possible difficulties do you think you can encounter when you ask for favors outside of your family?

....
....
....
....
....
....
....

b. list all you know about the importance of a good family

....
....
....
....
....
....
....
....
....
....
....

....
....
....
....
....

CROSS WORD

What do you think you should ask from the following people?

Match answer by drawing a line.

Uncle	Advice
Father	Books
Mother	Money
Friends	Spiritual guidance
Neighbours	Academic problems
Church leader	Clothes
Imam	Shoes
Aunty	Wristwatch
Siblings	School bag
Friends' sisters	Food
Father's friends	Socks
Mother's friends	Ice cream

Discuss your result

....
....
....
....
....
....
....
....
....
....
....

1.4   DEVELOPING A HAPPY FAMILY

For you to be a happy child you must come from a happy family, for you to come from a happy family you must make members of your family happy and vice versa. This you can do by being a good child and spending your time wisely.

1.4.1   BEING A GOOD CHILD

As a good child you have a duty of making your parents and other members of your family happy with you all the time. Also every member of your community must be pleased with your conduct at all times.

ACTIVITY

As a good child, what do you think are your responsibilities to your family and community as a whole?

....
....
....
....
....
....
....
....
....
....
....
....
....

1.4.1.1   RESPECT

As a good child you must be respectful to all people older than you especially adults. Yes! Adults include your security guards, house helps, cobblers, drivers, etc. This is a very important factor because most children only respect certain class of people. They despise the less privileged as lesser human beings so they talk to them anyhow. Some children even go as far as insulting and even beating house helps. This is very wrong. Your house-help probably has a child as old as you are, so the respect you accord your mother should be the same the house-help gets.

ACTIVITY

List the category of people you must respect.

....
....

....
....
....
....
....
....
....
....
....
....
....
....
....
....
....
....

SPENDING YOUR TIME WISELY

Time is limited. Because of this, a good child must cultivate the habit of **proper time management.**
It is very important to do the right thing at the right time.

We have 24 hours in a day: 15 hours of daylight and 9 hours of darkness.

As a good child you must spend the 15 hours available to you daily wisely on the following:

- Studying/doing homework after school
- Assisting your parents with household chores
- Developing a hobby
- Engaging in sporting activities like football, volley ball, table tennis etc.
- Attending religious activities
- Developing a time for siesta/rest

ACTIVITY

It is important to plan your day. What should you do at the following times?

6.00 a.m.	-	7.30 a.m.
7.30 a.m.	-	8.00 a.m.
8.00 a.m.	-	2.00 p.m.
2.30 pm	-	3.30 pm
4 p.m.	-	5 p.m.
5 p.m.	-	6 p.m.
6 p.m.	-	8 p.m.
8 p.m.	-	6 a.m.

1.4.1.2   Benefits of spending your time wisely

- You will enjoy good health and sound mind.
- You will have excellent performance in school.
- Your parents will be happy with you and will give you good gifts.
- You will become a role model to other children.
- You will become successful and a great man/woman in the future because children are the leaders of tomorrow.

1.4.1.3   NEVER

Play when you should be working or reading.
Never leave things you should do now for later, doing that is called **PROCRASTINATION.**
Procrastination is the thief of all time. Never procrastinate. Always remember the sayings that 'a stitch in time saves nine' and 'time lost is never regained'

ACTIVITY

1. Draw a time table showing how you would spend tomorrow.

2. Write a composition on the topic 'Time waits for no one.'

....
....
....
....
....
....
....
....
....
....
....
....

2.0 RELATIONSHIPS

A relationship can be defined as an interaction between two or more people, being together and interacting with one another at two different levels: blood relationship and friendship.

ACTIVITY

Who are your blood relations?

....
....
....
....
....

....
....

What are their duties to you?

....
....
....
....
....
....
....

Who is your friend?

....
....
....

What are the duties of your friend?

....
....
....
....
....
....
....
....
....
....
....

2.1 FRIENDSHIP

Your friends are those people who are not related to you by blood. Friendship is the state of attachment between people by bonds of affection, mutual respect and interest.

BASIS FOR FRIENDSHIP	BENEFITS OF FRIENDSHIP
Common interest	Companionship
Similar values	Love
Honesty	Protection
Loyalty	Support
Trust	Care

ACTIVITY

a. What do you understand by each of the parameters listed above?

....
....
....
....
....
....
....
....
....
....
....
....
....
....
....
....
....
....
....
....
....

b. List other basis and benefits of friendship not in the list above?

....
....
....
....
....

2.1.1 WAYS OF IMPROVING FRIENDSHIP

- Sharing information
- Exchanging visits and gifts
- Having group activities

ACTIVITY

List other ways of improving friendship that you know

....
....

....
....
....
....
....
....
....
....
....
....
....
....
....
....
....

Note that friendship

- is not falling in love
- is not having a sexual relationship
- is not selfishness
- is not visiting lonely or hidden places
- is not attending so many social functions, such as parties.

A good friend must be

- Respectful
- Responsible
- Understanding and
- Caring at all times
- Generous
- Must be giving and not selfish

ACTIVITY

'A friend in need is a friend indeed'. Write an essay on the statement.

....
....
....
....
....
....
....
....
....

....
....
....
....
....
....
....
....
....
....
....
....
....
....
....
....
....
....
....
....
....

2.2 FAMILY

At this point you are going to take a close look at your family. This will help you understand them because everyone is unique.

ACTIVITY

Draw a family tree comprising all members of your family.

Write down one thing about each member that makes them unique.

....
....
....
....
....
....
....
....
....
....

2.2.1 FAMILY CHANGES:

A family is usually not static, changes do occur over time. As you get older your parents also get older! Children always have a misconception that they alone need care. This is untrue because as parents age, they also encounter changes in their Health and Social lives.

- Some parents may suffer ill Health like hypertension, diabetes, poor sight, arthritis, liver failure and lung cancer

Some Social changes include:

- Children may go to boarding school
- Parents may be transferred from one town to another or one parent may have to move to work in another town.
- Parents may separate or get divorced
- Loss of a family member

For these reasons they also need you to show them love.

ACTIVITY

List some changes you have experienced in your family.

....
....
....
....
....
....
....
....
....

....
....
....
....
....

How did you cope with each change?

....
....
....
....
....
....
....
....
....
....
....
....
....
....
....
....
....
....

2.2.2   ADOLESCENCE

This is a period when a child reaches puberty usually between the ages of 10-19.

Most children do not know how to handle this period of change so they become rebellious because of a growing sense of independence, increased self awareness and responsibilities.

2.2.3   WAYS TO IMPROVE FAMILY FUNCTIONS INCLUDE:

- Show love
- cooperate with members of your family
- Show respect
- Communicate effectively

ACTIVITY

List other ways to improve family function

....
....
....
....
....
....
....
....
....
....
....
....
....
....

The best time I ever had with my family was:

....
....
....
....
....
....
....
....
....
....
....
....
....

Two customs in our family that I like are:

....
....
....
....
....
....
....

Children need families because:

....
....
....
....

2.3 LOVE

Love is a feeling of strong emotional attachment between people where there is respect and an attitude to encourage each other to develop as individuals.

2.3.1 FACTS AND MYTHS (True or False)

- Love is not the same as sexual involvement
- You can fall in love only once
- Love usually takes time to develop
- Love can only exist between persons of opposite sex

ACTIVITY

What do you understand by Love?

....
....
....
....
....
....
....
....

Have you ever been in love?

....

2.3.2 QUALITIES OF A GOOD LOVING RELATIONSHIP

- Mutual respect
- Mutual trust
- Encouragement
- Kindness
- Patience
- Sharing gifts
- Making plans together
- Attending social and religious functions together

ACTIVITY

Explain each point

....
....
....
....
....
....
....
....
....
....
....
....
....
....

2.4 DATING

This is a stage of a relationship that precedes marriage. It is a commitment usually between persons of opposite sex who are ready for marriage

2.4.1 REASONS FOR DATING

- Companionship
- Experience sharing
- Getting to understand each other
- Reading together
- Engaging in recreational activities
- Learning about each other in terms of strengths and weaknesses

2.4.2 RISKS IN DATING

- Distraction from school work
- Pressure to go against family or personal values
- Emotional and peer pressure
- Sexual involvement
- HIV/AIDS
- Rape
- Introduction to drugs, smoking or alcohol
- Cultism, robbery and other social ills

Dating is not for children and adolescents but for adults considering marriage because of the great risk involved

ACTIVITY

At what age should you consider dating and why?

....
....
....
....

2.5 MARRIAGE

This is a social and legal commitment that a man and woman make to come together as husband and wife and share their lives and family responsibilities

Activity
What are married people called?

....
....

2.5.1   ROLES AND RESPONSIBILITIES OF MARRIED COUPLES

Companionship
Security
Reproduction
Parenting
Financial provision

2.5.2   CHARACTERISTICS OF A HAPPY MARRIAGE

Shared values
Commitment
Honesty
Mutual support
Similarity of goals

2.5.3   IMPLICATIONS OF DIVORCE

Battle over children's custody
Lack of proper parenting of children
Emotional trauma for both children and parents

Activity
List some other implications of divorce you know

....
....
....
....
....
....
....

2.6   TEENAGE MARRIAGE

A teenager is someone between the ages of thirteen and nineteen.
This is a marriage between a teenager and an older person or between two teenagers.

2.6.1   IMPLICATIONS OF TEENAGE MARRIAGE

- Inability to complete Education
- Incidence of wife/child abuse
- Vesico vaginal fistulae(VVF)
- Improper parenting

ACTIVITY

Would you like to get married as a teenager?

....
....

Explain your reason.

....
....
....
....
....
....
....
....
....

2.7 PARENTING

Parental responsibilities mean the obligations of parents towards their children. It includes

- Financial provision
- Material provision
- Food security
- Guidance and bringing up children
- Support and care of whatever forms that will help the development of the children

Activity
What are the challenges of working parents?

....
....
....
....
....
....
....

What are cultural variations in parenting? (Research based)

....
....
....
....
....
....
....
....
....
....
....
....
....
....

2.8   RELATIONSHIP WITH LARGER SOCIETY

In relating with people in the society generally you must do the right thing always!

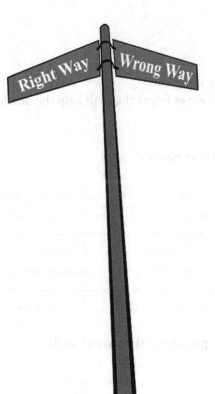

- Never forget the use of the basic words, please, thank you and sorry where you have caused offence
- Always answer your elders saying Ma or Sir
- If you hurt anyone say sorry
- If you want to borrow anything from anyone start by saying 'please may I'
- Do not be rude to people
- Do not take things without permission from their owner
- Tell the truth always
- Do not be a bad influence to other children in your neighborhood
- Do not quarrel
- Do not steal
- Do not fight
- Make your bed immediately you wake up
- Keep your clothes well folded in your wardrobe and boxes
- Do not litter the environment by throwing rubbish out of a moving car or on the floor. Always throw rubbish in the dustbin.

CHAPTER THREE

3.0   GROWING UP AND HUMAN DEVELOPMENT

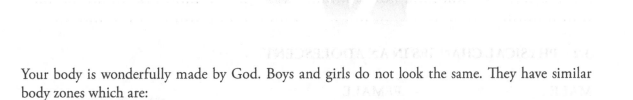

Your body is wonderfully made by God. Boys and girls do not look the same. They have similar body zones which are:

Red – This is the sensitive part of your body and you must not allow anyone to touch it.

Green – These are the exposed parts of your body

Yellow – This means warning. These parts are close to the sensitive parts and must not be touched.

ACTIVITY

What are the functions of the different parts of your body?

....
....
....
....
....
....
....
....

....
....
....
....
....

3.1   CHANGES THAT OCCOUR DURING ADOLESCENCE

When a child is growing up there are changes that occur in him or her. These changes are normal and are signs that the boy or girl is becoming an adult. This is the period of adolescence and puberty.

Activity
Define an adolescent

....
....
....
....
....
....
....

3.2   PHYSICAL CHANGES IN AN ADOLESCENT

MALE	FEMALE
Pimples	Pimples
Facial hairs	Armpit/Pubic hair
Broad chest	Enlargement of breast
Armpit hair/Pubic hair	Narrowing of waist
Wet dreams	Enlargement of hips
Cracking of voice	Menstruation
Muscles	

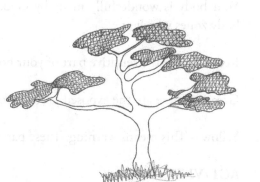

NOTE THAT:

During adolescence you may sweat a lot. This can lead to pimples and body odour. Hence you must be very clean and bath regularly.

Others like social and emotional changes can not be seen. They include:

1. wanting to make decisions
2. being independent

ACTIVITY
List other social and emotional changes you know or have experienced.

....
....
....
....
....
....
....

3.3   MENSTRUATION

- This occurs when a girl is approaching adulthood. This is natural and is preparing her for womanhood.
- Menstruation is the flow of blood from the vagina and it occurs once in a month and lasts for 2 to 7 days
- Once a girl starts to menstruate she can get pregnant if she has sexual intercourse with a matured boy or a man. This might make her drop out of school hence she must not experiment with sex because it is dangerous and can make her ruin her future. She must ABSTAIN
- During menstruation you must be clean and change sanitary towels regularly to prevent infection
- It is a natural thing to menstruate; it is not an illness but an indication that you can have children.
- A girl that does not menstruate must see a health practitioner because she may not be able to have children in the future.

3.3.1   THINGS EXPERIENCED BY A GIRL DURING MENSTRUATION

- Pain in the lower abdomen
- Headache
- Slight fever
- Brest pain/tenderness
- Bad mood
- Diarrhea /constipation

3.3.2   WHAT TO DO

- Discuss with your mother or teacher but not with your friends because they may give you wrong information
- Keep yourself very clean to prevent infection
- Do exercise
- Eat plenty of fruits and take plenty of water

- Do not use perfume or powder on the vagina during menstruation because it can cause irritation and itching
- Carry out your daily activities normally

3.4 WET DREAM

This is a major sign of approaching manhood for the young boy.

A wet dream is when an adolescent boy wakes up from bed and notices that his pant or bed is wet. This is different from wetting the bed with urine called enuresis.

Once a boy starts to have wet dreams he can impregnate a girl or woman if he has sexual intercourse with her. This can destroy his future.

It is a natural thing to have wet dreams; it is not an illness but an indication that you can have children

3.4.1 WHAT THE BOY SHOULD DO

- He should not be worried or ashamed.
- He can discuss it with parents or teacher but not with friends because they may give wrong information
- He should wash his bed sheets and clothes immediately.
- He should abstain from sexual intercourse
- He should carry out daily activities normally

ACTIVITY

Summarize what you understand by menstruation and wet dreams.

....
....
....
....
....
....
....
....
....
....
....
....
....
....

....
....
....
....
....
....
....
....
....
....
....
....
....
....
....
....
....
....
....
....
....
....
....

4.0   HIV/AIDS AND SEXUAL HEALTH

At this point you know all about sex and know that sex is not a social past time. Sex is not for children. We will now deal with diseases that could arise as a result of sex. These are called sexually transmitted Infections (STIs) and HIV/AIDS

Know your abbreviations

STI: Sexually Transmitted Infection
HIV: Human Immunodeficiency Virus
AIDS: Acquired Immune Deficiency Syndrome
MTCT: Mother to Child Transmission
PLWHA: People Living with HIV/AIDS

4.1   WHAT IS HIV/AIDS?

AIDS is caused by a tiny germ called Human immunodeficiency virus, simply put HIV. HIV is the most deadly of all the infections that one can get through sex because it has no cure for now.

Important note:

HIV is not only gotten through sex

Other ways of getting the infection:

1. By sharing needles, blades and other sharp instruments which have been used by an infected person
2. by receiving blood transfusion from someone who is infected with HIV
3. from mother to an unborn child and or during breast feeding

4.1.1   ONE CANNOT GET INFECTED WITH HIV

- By playing working and living together
- By shaking hands
- By sharing cups and plates
- From eating together
- Through mosquito/insect bites
- Through coughing and sneezing

4.1.2   COMMON MYTHS ABOUT HIV/AIDS

- Punishment from God
- American invention to discourage sex
- Sleeping with virgins can cure AIDS
- HIV can be contracted from sharing Public toilets
- Mosquitoes can transmit HIV

4.1.3   HIV TRANSMISSION

The virus is found in the following body fluids of an infected person

- Semen
- Vaginal discharge
- Blood
- Breast milk
- Saliva

Transmission occurs where there is contact with these fluids through any of the following means

- Unprotected sexual intercourse (genitals, anally or orally)
- Unscreened blood transfusion
- Sharing contaminated skin piercing instruments like needles, razor blade, clippers etc
- Mother to child transmission (in uterus, during labor and delivery and during breast feeding)
- Kissing

4.1.4 SOME SIGNS AND SYMPTOMS OF HIV/AIDS

- Weight loss
- Persistent chronic diarrhea
- Recurrent fever
- Severe bacterial infection
- Persistent cough lasting over a month
- Generalized lymphadenopathy
- Recurrent Herpes zoster

4.1.5 HIV PREVENTION CAN BE ACHIEVED BY

- Abstinence A
- Being faithful B
- Consistent and correct condom usage C
- Insisting on screened blood transfusion
- Avoidance of contact with any contaminated sharp objects like blades, clippers, needles etc
- Prevention of mother to child transmission (PMTCT)

4.1.6 BENEFITS OF TESTING FOR STI AND HIV

- Early detection, treatment and care
- Builds confidence
- Helps in prevention by facilitating behavior change

4.1.7 POSITIVE LIVING FOR PLWHAS

PLWHAS is an acronym for people living with HIV/AIDS. Positive living refers to the life style that is appropriate for one who test positive to HIV to enable him/her continue to live well normally and reduce the risk of further re-infection. They include

- proper nutrition
- Avoiding exposure to all other illness
- Avoid alcohol, cigarettes, drug abuse etc
- Prompt treatment of any illness
- Avoidance of re-infection through any risky behavior
- Adequate rest

4.1.8 IMPACT OF HIV/AIDS

HIV/AIDS impacts on individuals, families, communities, the workplace, schools and the entire nation in a number of ways

- It affects both personal, family and community finance
- The work force: loss of skilled and experienced manpower

- Pressure on already overworked health care providers
- Children have to run families due to loss of parents to AIDS

Activity

What will you do if you meet anybody infected with the virus?

....
....
....
....
....
....
....
....
....
....
....
....
....

4.2   SIGNS AND SYPTOMS OF STIs

For men

- A wound, sore, ulcer, rash and blisters on or around the penis
- Discharge and pus from the penis
- Pain or burning feeling when passing urine
- Pain and swelling of the testis

For women

- Thick, itchy, foul smelling discharge from the vagina
- Pain during sexual intercourse
- Abnormal irregular bleeding from the vagina

4.3   SEXUAL ABUSE

This is any form of unwanted sexual attention or intercourse by an older person to a younger person. Examples are rape and sexual harassment

What can lead to sexual abuse?

Anything! Some examples are
Hugging with the opposite sex in isolated places
Dressing provocatively
Leaving children in the company of sexually perverted individuals

Where can sexual abuse occur?

Anywhere! At home, school, work place etc

Who is likely to commit sexual abuse?

Anyone! Friends, relatives, teachers, bosses in the office, colleagues and parents

4.4 RAPE

This is sexual assault committed with violence or threat that culminates in sexual intercourse

4.4.1 Causes of rape

- Emotional force (sexual)
- Psychological (e.g. need for power or the tendency to dominate)

4.4.2 Myths about rape

A woman deserves to be raped if she dresses provocatively
Only women/girls are raped
A person can not be raped by someone known to him or her
A wife cannot be raped by her husband
A man cannot be raped by a woman

4.4.3 Types of pain faced by rape victims

Psychological pain/mental abuse
Physical pain
Fear of rejection

Activity

How do you think that rape can be avoided?

....

....

....

....
....
....
....
....

4.5   SEXUAL HARASSMENT

This is any form of unwanted sexual solicitation including

- Touching
- Obscene telephone calls/communication
- Comments
- Whistling
- Gestures like rolling of tongue
- A male teacher inviting female students for outing or vice versa

Activity

What will you do if someone harasses you sexually?

....
....
....
....
....
....
....
....
....

4.6   SEXUAL RELATIONSHIP

This is an intimate relationship between married couples involving the use of penis and vagina.

Note

Even if I see people having sex on TV, hear it on the radio or by my friends, I must not have sex because

- I may get painful diseases such as gonorrhea, syphilis, herpes, HIV
- My body is not fully developed to have sex
- I am not ready to become a father or a mother
- I will not be able to finish my studies
- It will bring shame to me and my family

- I will be removed from social groups I belong to in my school, neighborhood and religious institutions
- I may become an errand boy or girl to those who completed their education

Always say 'NO' to sex

Activity

What will you do if anyone pressurizes you to have sex?

....
....
....
....
....
....

How to say 'NO'

Say NO and leave the place
Say NO and give reasons e.g. I am not matured now, we are not married yet e.t.c
Say NO while looking into the person's eye
Don't receive gifts suggesting or influencing you to have sex
Dress decently at all times

Activity

Suggest other ways of saying 'NO'

....
....
....
....
....
....
....

5. PERSONAL SKILLS:

5.0 VALUES

These are ideas, beliefs and qualities that are dear to us, important and desirable to the point of influencing our conduct or character.

They are important because we are usually the outcome of our values. We act according to what we value.

5.0.1 IMPORTANCE OF VALUES

Give meaning and direction to life.
Enhance dignity.
Help in decision-making.

5.0.2 EXAMPLES OF NATIONAL VALUES ARE:

1. Discipline.
2. Honesty.
3. Dignity of labor.

4. Respect.
5. Hard work.
6. Patriotism

5.0.3 FACTORS THAT INFLUENCE OUR VALUES ARE:

- Family
- Peers
- Community
- Religion
- Media
- Personal experience

5.0.4 EFFECTS OF VALUES

When upheld

- Feeling good
- Sense of fulfillment
- Improved self esteem

When not upheld

- Guilt
- Conflict
- Discomfort
- Shame
- indifference

Activity

a. What personal values can you attribute to your life?

....
....
....
....
....
....
....
....
....
....

b. Develop and write a Mission Statement that will guide your activities in life

....
....

....
....
....
....
....
....
....

5.1 SELF ESTEEM

Self esteem is simply valuing oneself and not looking down on oneself. It also means accepting both your strengths and weaknesses

5.1.0 FACTORS THAT INFLUENCE SELF ESTEEM:

1. Upbringing
2. Accomplished goals
3. Bad company

5.1.1 TYPES OF SELF ESTEEM

1. High self esteem: When a person recognizes and accepts both his strengths and weaknesses.
2. Low self esteem: When a person only sees his/her shortcomings and weaknesses and sees nothing good in his/her self.

5.1.2 CHARACTERISTICS OF SELF ESTEEM

1. **High self esteem**: The person is confident, has the ability to relate well with others, resist peer pressure and has the ability to make decisions for his or her self.
2. **Low self esteem**: Lack of confidence, isolation, 'follow – follow' and unsociable.

Activity

a. Do you have self esteem?
b. Tick your characteristics from the list below

HIGH	LOW
Confident – humble	Arrogant and gossips
Assertive, Discuss ideas openly	Critical of others
Interactive	Rebellious withdrawal and isolation
Caring attitude	Inferiority complex
Respect for authority	Allows self to be pushed around, ineffective

c. How would you rate your self esteem?

....
....
....
....
....
....
....
....
....
....
....
....

d. What is the link between self esteem and values?

....
....
....
....
....
....
....
....
....
....
....
....
....
....
....

5.2   GOAL SETTING:

Goals are the things/ target we want to achieve in life, which we direct our energy and resources towards. Goal setting is the process of determining a goal/goals, planning and working towards it.

5.2.0   IMPORTANACNE OF GOAL SETTING

It gives direction
It helps in planning to be organized

Activity

a. What are your goals in life?

....
....
....
....
....
....
....
....
....
....
....

b. How do you intend to achieve these goals?

....
....
....
....
....
....
....
....
....
....
....
....
....
....
....

5.2.1 TYPES OF GOAL SETTING

    a. Daily goals setting or short term goals
    b. Monthly goal setting
    c. Yearly goal setting or long term goals

You continuously set goals for yourself else you lose focus.

Activity

a. Write out your long term goals and your short term goals.

....
....
....
....
....
....

Recopy from your book to a piece of paper and place it where you can always see it.

b. What is the link between self esteem, values and goal setting?

....
....
....
....
....
....
....
....

5.2.2 SOME DIFFICULTIES EXPERIENCED IN SETTING GOALS FOR THE FUTURE ARE:

1. Pessimistic attitude
2. Lack of ambition
3. Procrastination
4. Low self esteem
5. Ignorance of the importance of goal setting

5.2.3 SOME BARRIERS TO ACHIEVING GOALS ARE:

1. Teenage pregnancy
2. STI, HIV/AIDS
3. Bad company
4. Lack of information

5.2.4   SOME EFFECTS OF ACHIEVING GOALS ARE:

1. Increased self esteem
2. Motivation
3. Feeling of achievement

5.3   DECISION MAKING

This is the process of making up our mind on an issue or solution and taking a position on it.

5.3.0   STEPS INVOLVED IN DECISION MAKING

1. Recognize the decision to be made
2. List all possible choices
3. Weigh the "pros" and "cons" of each other choice
4. Examine your decision
5. Make the decision
6. Review the decision (choice)

ACTIVITY

Follow the steps listed above to make any decision you choose

....
....
....
....
....
....
....
....
....
....
....
....
....
....
....
....

5.3.1   DIFFICULTIES YOUNG PEAPLE FACE ABOUT DECISION MAKING

1. Peer pressure
2. Lack of decision making skills

3. Drugs and alcohol
4. Lack of access to adequate information and facts
5. Lack of access to trusted and experienced persons

5.3.2 POSSIBLE BARRIERS TO IMPLEMENTING DECISIONS

- Peer pressure
- Poor planning
- Decision not consistent with set goals or values

5.3.3 HOW TO OVERCOME THESE BARRIERS:

- Take decisions that are in line with your set goals or values in life.
- Be goal oriented
- Have a time limit
- Develop refusal and negotiation skills
- Make proper plans
- Take action

Activity

What major decision have you made in your life? And how did you go about it. Explain the difficulties you encountered and the barriers you faced in implementing your decision

....
....
....
....
....
....
....
....
....
....
....
....
....
....
....
....
....
....
....

....
....
....
....
....
....
....
....
....
....
....
....

5.3.4   STRATEGIES FOR AVOIDING REPEATED MISTAKES:

1. Evaluate past decisions and outcomes and learn from them
2. Patience
3. Think positively

5.3.5   CHARACTERISTICS OF A GOOD DECISION

1. Goal oriented
2. Consistent with values (personal values)
3. Based on correct information and facts from experts in that area

5.3.6   FACTOERS THAT INFLUENCE DECISION ABOUT SEXUALITY

1. Sexual feelings of the individual
2. Religion
3. Society
4. Media
5. Drugs
6. Alcohol
7. Economics
8. Ignorance

5.3.7   EFFECTS OF DECISIONS ABOUT SEXUALITY

Good decision about sexuality will have positive effects/ impacts on us. While bad decision on the other hand will have negative effects on us. The following areas of our life can be directly or indirectly affected by our decision on sexuality.

1. Emotional/Psychological life
2. Sexual life
3. Economic life

---

4. Educational life
5. Spiritual life
6. Career life

5.3.8. SEXUAL LIMITS IN RELATIONHIPS AND RISK ASSOCIATED WITH PREMARITAL/ UNPROTECTED SEX.

1. Unwanted pregnancy (unplanned)
2. STI'S
3. HIV/AIDS
4. Sexual exploitation
5. Loss of self (esteem) respect

Activity:

What is your decision in life concerning sexuality?

......

44

....
....
....
....
....
....
....
....

5.4   COMMUNICATION:

Communication is the process by which a message is transferred from one person to another or a group using verbal or non verbal means.

5.4.0   THE COMMUNICATION PROCESS

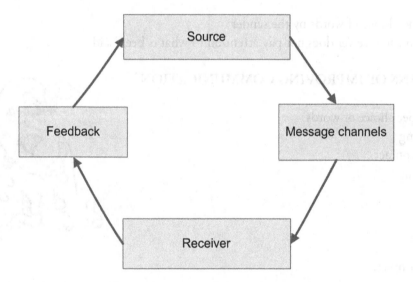

5.4.1   CHARACTERISTICS OF GOOD COMMUNICATION

1. Careful listening
2. Clear speaking
3. Proper use of verbal and non – verbal skills

Activity

a. What do you understand by verbal and non-verbal communication?

....
....
....

....
....
....
....

b. From your knowledge about communication, can you define miscommunication?

....
....
....
....
....
....
....

5.4.2   CAUSES OF MISCOMMUNICATION

1. Wrong choice of words by the sender
2. When the receiver does not pay attention to what is been said

5.4.3   MEANS OF IMPROVING COMMUNICATION

Correct/ proper choice of words
Active listening
Making eye contact
Understanding
Observing

Activity:

List other examples:

....
....
....
....
....
....

5.4.4   BEHAVIOURS THAT IMPAIR COMMUNICATION ARE:

• Not listening
• Yelling or talking loudly
• Blaming, Criticism
• Interrupting
• Negative non – verbal means e.g. frowning

5.4.5   FACTORS THAT CAN CAUSE DIFFERENCES IN MEANING

- Personality.
- Gender
- Cultural background
- Educational background

5.4.6   BARRIERS TO COMMUNCATION ABOUT SEXUALITY

- Improper training/Non availability of training
- Religious values
- Cultural values/ Taboos

5.4.7   STRATEGIES FOR IMPROVING COMMUNICATION ON SEXUALITY

- Sexual terms desensitization
- Values and values clarification

Activity

List other strategies:

....
....
....
....
....
....
....
....

5.5   ASSERTIVENESS

This means standing up for your right or what you believe in without violating someone else's rights.

5.5.0   BARRIERS TO FEMALES BEING ASSERTIVE INCLUDE

1. Religion
2. Culture
3. Ignorance
4. Male dominance

Activity

Discuss myths about gender roles

....
....
....
....
....
....
....
....
....
....
....
....
....
....
....

5.5.1 RIGHTS THAT SUPPORT ASSERTIVENESS ARE:

- Right to have views and express them
- Right of choice
- Right to fair treatment/hearing and not be intimidated

Note:

You must uphold rules and regulations of your school, home and society at large.

5.5.2 BEHAVOIURS THAT IMPROVE ASSERTIVENESS

- Honesty
- Uprightness
- Quickly expressing or communicating feelings/needs as they come up rather than waiting.

5.5.3 BENEFITS OF ASSERTIVNESS AGAINST SEXUAL ABUSE SITUATIONS:

- Prevention of sexual exploitation
- Prevention of unwanted pregnancy
- Prevention of STI, HIV/AIDS
- Taking responsibility for ones feelings or needs

5.5.4 CONSEQUENCIES OF NON – ASSERTIVENESS IN SEXUAL ABUSE SITUATIONS:

1. Pregnancy
2. Diseases can cause damage to sexual organs and infertility
3. Sexual exploitation
4. Unhappiness/dissatisfaction
5. Feeling hurt

Activity

Have you ever been assertive?

....

Discuss an instance.

....
....
....
....
....
....
....
....

5.6   NEGOTIATION

This is a process that leads to amicable agreement or disagreement by two or more people on how to solve a problem. The process involves the ability to compromise. This way, one's goals are met without guilt or hurting the next person. The best time to negotiate is when a problem or conflict is addressed in the early stage.

5.6.0   EFFECTS OF GOOD NEGOTIATION

1. Promotes good relationship
2. Promotes mutual respect
3. Creates understanding

5.6.1   EFFECTIVE NEGOTIATION SKILLS

1. Listening effectively
2. Careful observation
3. Identifying all the options in a given situation
4. Imagining oneself in the other persons position

5. Appropriate use of verbal and non-verbal communication skills
6. Willingness to make a compromise

5.6.2 NEGOTIATION TECHNIQUES: These can be summarized by the acronym SWAT

S - Say NO effectively
W - Give the Why (reason) for your position
A - Give an Alternative
T - Take it out

Important note:

SWAT also means Special Weapons and Tactics

Activity:

What is the importance of negotiation?

……
……
……
………………………………………………………………………………………

5.6.3 FINDING HELP

Teenagers and/or young people generally get bothered and may require help in the following circumstances.

1. Confusion resulting from conflict over societal/family values
2. Concerns over changes in the body, particularly pubertal changes
3. Emotional and social concerns
4. Peer pressure

5.6.4 PEOPLE/ORGANISATIONS THAT COULD BE OF HELP ARE:

1. Counselors
2. Religious leaders
3. Trusted experienced adults
4. Non Governmental Organizations
5. Community Based Organizations
6. Youth centers

5.6.5 CHARACTERISTICS OF SUCH PEOPLE/ORGANIZATIONS

1. Respect for confidentiality

2. Cost little or no money
3. Know when and how to involve parents

5.6.6 STEPS TO TAKE WHEN SEEKING HELP

1. Try to think
2. be careful
3. Stay focused
4. Go straight to identified help center/person

Activity

Is there any issue bothering you? Do you need any form of help? Discuss the problem.

....
....
....
....
....
....
....
....
....
....
....
....
....
....
....
....
....
....
....
....
....

5.7 REFUSAL SKILLS

Refusal is the ability to clearly say No to or show that one is unwilling to do, give or accept what the other person is requesting.

In refusal, the response is No and it is clear, simple and straightforward while in negotiation, there is compromise. The best time to use refusal skill is when you do not want what is being suggested or requested of you.

5.7.0   FACTORS THAT HELP REFUSAL:

1.   High self esteem
2.   Having a goal
3.   Good communication skills
4.   Assertiveness.

Activity

Explain how each factor listed above helps refusal.

....
....
....
....
....
....
....
....
....
....
....
....
....
....

NOTE:

When you say NO, keep saying NO and don't bother to offer an explanation. Refuse to discuss the matter and walk away if that is the only option left.

CHAPTER SIX

SEXUAL BEHAVIOUR

6.0   SEX

This refers to the biological state of being male or female. It is also sometimes used to refer to having intercourse.

6.1   ABSTINENCE

This is when a person for whatever reason, decides to completely stay away from having any form of sexual intercourse.

6.1.0   TYPES OF ABSTINENCE

1. Life long abstinence
2. Periodic abstinence is from time to time
3. Secondary abstinence: for persons who were sexually active but at a point decided to stop

6.1.1   ADVANTAGES OF ABSTINENCE

1. Best form of prevention against unwanted pregnancy, STI and HIV/AIDS
2. Allows teenagers to concentrate on their education
3. Promote respect for people's sexual rights

6.2   RELIGIOUS INJUNCTIONS ABOUT PRE-MARITAL SEX

The dominant religions in Nigeria (Christianity and Islam) promote sexual chastity before and within marriage. It is important for people to practice what their religion teaches about sexual chastity as disobedience is not only a sin against God but also exposes us to many dangers like unwanted pregnancy, STI, HIV/AIDS.

Activity

From personal skills learnt in chapter five, in that format write out your decision about abstinence.

....
....
....

....
....
....
....
....
....
....
....
....
....
....
....
....
....
....
....
....
....
....
....
....
....
....
....
....
....
....
....
....
....

6.3 SEXUALITY:

Is the way we feel about ourselves and the way we express ourselves in friendship, etc.

Sex differs from sexuality in the sense that sex refers to a state while sexuality has to do with FEELINGS and EXPRESSION

Activity

CROSS WORD:	**AGE (YEARS)**
1. Has a sense of being male/female	15
2. Falls in love	20
3. May masturbate	30
4. Begin dating	50
5. Has friends of same sex	70
6. Has friends of opposite sex	40
7. Is able to have a child	60
8. Goes to work and takes on responsibilities	55
9. Feels awkward and wonders "am I normal?"	10
10. Can no longer bear children	5

CHAPTER SEVEN

7.0   DRUG/ SUBSTANCE ABUSE

At this period of your life you are still in the process of forming your behavior patterns hence can be most likely influenced by your peers and role models. You have probably taken a medication (drug) to treat an illness or seen someone smoking a cigarette (substance).

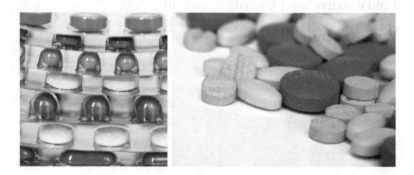

7.1   WHAT IS A DRUG/SUBSTANCE?

A drug can be defined as a natural or synthetic **substance** which when taken into a living body affects its functioning and structure. From this definition it is clear that a drug could also be referred to as a substance

Narcotic substances produce a state of arousal, contentment or euphoria. Such substances are habit forming and can cause **addiction or dependence**

7.2   ADDICTION OR DEPENDENCE

This can be defined as an overdependence on and compulsive craving for a drug mostly a habit forming stimulant or a narcotic substance. Discontinuation of this substance causes specific reactions called **withdrawal symptoms**

7.2.1   WITHDRAWAL SYMPTOMS

This is a reaction that occurs when a drug addict discontinues the use of the substance. Some of the symptoms are:

1. Sweating
2. Vomiting
3. Tremors
4. Anger
5. Irritability
6. Depression
7. Muscle cramps

7.3   WHAT DRUGS ARE MEANT FOR

Drugs are meant for the relief of discomfort hence it is used in management of diseases or illness for:

- Diagnosis
- Mitigation,
- Treatment
- Prevention

7.4   WHAT IS DRUG/SUBSTANCE ABUSE?

This can be defined as

1. The use of illegal drugs
2. The misuse of prescription and over the counter drugs
3. A compulsive, excessive and self damaging use of habit forming drugs or substances

Usually the person becomes dependent in order to get through each day

7.5   NAMES AND TYPES OF COMMON DRUGS/SUBSTANCES OF ABUSE

7.5.1   Narcotic substances such as

- Alcohol e.g. wine, beer, spirits, home brew
- Cannabis e.g. marijuana, ganja, hashish, bhang, weed
- Nicotine e.g. cigarettes, cigars, pipe, tobacco, snuff

7.5.2   Drugs such as

- Sleeping pills e.g. Diazepam
- Anti-depressants
- Narcotic analgesics e.g. codeine, Heroine, morphine, opium, methadone, pethidine
- Steroids

Activity

List other names of drugs/substance you know of

....

....

....

7.6   EFFECTS OF DRUG OR SUBSTANCE ABUSE

1. Smoking may lead to lung cancer
2. May cause damage to kidneys, liver and heart
3. Dysfunctional behavior patterns
4. Hallucinations
5. Memory loss or black outs
6. Loss of self control
7. Depression
8. Anxiety
9. Shame
10. Disqualification from performing sports
11. Death
12. Legal implications and Imprisonment
13. Accidents
14. Isolation

7.7   FACTORS THAT CAN INFLUENCE DRUG ABUSE

1. A lack of attachment and nurturing by parents or caregivers
2. Ineffective parenting or parental neglect
3. A caregiver who abuses drugs
4. Association with drug-abusing peer
5. Curiosity
6. Lack of life building skills
7. Environmental factors

7.8   LIFE SKILLS TO PREVENT DRUG ABUSE

1. Be assertive and resist peer pressure
2. Practice your refusal skills
3. Find help
4. Families can provide protection from later drug abuse when there is:

•   A strong bond between children and parents
•   Parental involvement in the child's life
•   Clear limits and consistent enforcement of discipline

8. MALARIA

Malaria is a serious disease because it has been reported to be the second leading cause of death in Africa and the fifth cause of death worldwide (Centers for disease control website 2011). In general, malaria is a curable disease if diagnosed and treated promptly and correctly.

Activity:

Have you ever had malaria?

………………………………………………………………………………………………………

………………………………………………………………………………………………………

………………………………………………………………………………………………………

………………………………………………………………………………………………………

8.1 TYPES OF MALARIA

Malaria is categorized as

1. Uncomplicated Malaria
2. Severe malaria also called complicated Malaria

8.2 CAUSE OF MALARIA

Malaria is a parasitic disease caused by a parasite that commonly infects a certain type of mosquito called the **female *Anopheles* mosquito** which feeds on human blood. The parasite transmitted is called **Plasmodium**. There are different species of this parasite.

8.3 SOME CHARACTERISTICS OF THE FEMALE *ANOPHELES* MOSQUITO

- Your parents probably do not allow you to go out in the night. One of the reasons is to protect you from this mosquito because they are usually active in the evening/night time and rest during the day
- Mosquito larvae grow in stagnant water
- Mosquitoes are attracted to dark colored clothing

Activity:

Have you ever had a mosquito bite during the day?

....

....

8.4   SIGNS AND SYMPTOMS OF MALARIA

People who get malaria may have the following symptoms
Fever
High body temperature
Chills
Flu-like illness
Headache
Sweats,
Muscle pain
Nausea
Vomiting
Joint pain

8.5   MALARIA DIAGNOSIS

Malaria can be diagnosed by

- Clinical diagnosis
- Laboratory diagnosis

8.5.1   CLINICAL DIAGNOSIS

Clinical diagnosis is based on the patient's symptoms and on physical findings at examination

8.5.2   LABORATORY DIAGNOSIS

Laboratory diagnosis is usually done using a Microscope or a Rapid Diagnostic test (RDT) kit

8.6   TREATMENT OF MALARIA

When you have been diagnosed to have malaria ensure that you use all the medications you are given by your Health care provider as directed. Do not misuse anti malarial drugs because such a practice can lead to drug resistance by malaria-causing parasite thereby rendering such drugs ineffective or useless.

8.7 PREVENTION OF MALARIA

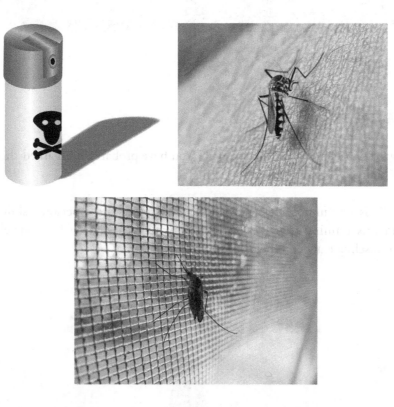

Malaria can be prevented by:

Sleeping under insecticide treated bed nets (ITNs)
Preventive treatment in pregnant women
Indoor residual spraying
Ensure that there is proper drainage and no collection of stagnant water around your house
Use of insecticide and larvicide
Window screens or nets
Light colored clothing
Long skirts and trousers with long sleeved shirts

Activity

List other methods you think can be used to prevent Malaria

....
....
....
....
....
....
....

CHAPTER NINE

CHOOSING A CAREER

What do you want to become when you grow up? You have probably been asked this question many times and as a child you naturally keep wondering.

What to do in life is very important hence you have to apply all the personal skill and other skills you acquired in this training to achieve the career you have chosen for yourself. Talk to your guidance and counseling teacher to help you.

How to choose the
Best Career for yourself ?

Below are some questions to help you find your passion.

What subjects do you enjoy most?

....
....
....
....
....
....

What sports do you enjoy?

....
....
....
....
....
....

Do you enjoy intensive reading or just a little reading?

....
....
....
....
....
....

How many hours do you study daily?

....
....
....
....
....
....

Do you love watching movies?

....
....
....
....
....
....

What are your hobbies?

....
....
....
....
....
....

Do you enjoy dancing, singing, acting drama?

....
....
....
....
....
....

Do you like to observe things?

....
....
....
....
....
....

Do you ask questions about everything and not be satisfied until you find the answer?

....
....
....
....
....
....

Do you love cooking and eating?

....
....
....
....
....
....

Do you love playing or watching football?

....
....
....
....
....
....

Do you like talking to people?

....
....
....
....
....
....

Do you love sick people?

....
....
....
....
....
....

Do you love traveling?

....
....
....
....
....
....

What do you think you will enjoy doing as a profession, i.e. what will you like to become in future?

Write an essay detailing how you will achieve this ambition.

....
....
....
....
....
....
....
....
....
....
....
....

....
....
....
....
....
....
....
....
....
....
....
....
....
....
....

The menace of sexual promiscuity and drug addiction has Social, Economic and Political implications for individuals, Society and Nation.

When you say 'NO' to premarital sex and drugs you will not only safeguard your body and soul, you will also realize the full potential of your God- given endowments in life in terms of Academics, Sports, Music, the Arts, the Sciences etc

You will thereby contribute your own quota to societal development, growth and advancement of Humanity and that is the whole essence of life!

So, make your parents proud of you by shunning all forms of vices today!!

God bless you as you read this book and allow the contents abide in you.

With lots of love from

Habibat Onyioza Sheidu